1 MONTH OF
FREE
READING

at

www.ForgottenBooks.com

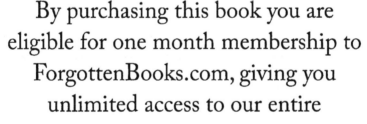

By purchasing this book you are
eligible for one month membership to
ForgottenBooks.com, giving you
unlimited access to our entire
collection of over 1,000,000 titles via
our web site and mobile apps.

To claim your free month visit:

www.forgottenbooks.com/free699270

ISBN 978-0-483-94745-0
PIBN 10699270

RELIGION AND PHILOSOPHY UNITED:

OR,

AN ATTEMPT TO SHOW THAT PHILOSOPHICAL PRINCIPLES
LIE AT THE FOUNDATION OF THE
NEW JERUSALEM CHURCH.

Margaret Hiller

BY

MRS. M. H. PRESCOTT.

SECOND EDITION.

WITH A MEMOIR OF THE AUTHOR,

BY HER SON,

REV. O. PRESCOTT HILLER.

LONDON:
WILLIAM WHITE, 36, BLOOMSBURY STREET.
BOSTON: OTIS CLAPP, 3, BEACON STREET.
1856.

GLASGOW:
PRINTED BY BELL AND BAIN.

PREFACE TO THE SECOND EDITION.

THE first edition of the following little work was published at Boston, United States, in the year 1817, and has been long out of print. On arriving in this country, I was gratified at finding copies in the libraries of several English Newchurchmen, one of whom was the late Mr. Noble. The name of the author was not, however, generally known, as it was not affixed to the original edition. A possessor of one of the copies, a Minister of the Church, on learning that the work was by my mother, warmly urged me to re-publish it. The idea had previously occurred to myself, but was much strengthened by a recommendation from such a quarter. I felt, moreover, in a manner, constrained by a sense of filial duty, to undertake it; and I may frankly add, that, after a careful perusal of the work in my mature years, its intrinsic value seemed to me a sufficient reason for its re-publication. It is *not*, *perhaps*, becoming in a son to speak too strongly in this regard; yet, when, in particular, the period of its publication is considered, it will, I think, be pronounced a work of more than ordinary literary merit. At that time, few, comparatively, of the collateral works of the Church had been published. Mr. Noble's "Appeal'" and other excellent works had not yet appeared; and, in America, so far as I am aware, nothing whatever of the kind had been written. So that this little work stands among the very beginnings of New Church literature, and from that circumstance alone possesses a certain value, which will be enhanced with the progress of time. It may be added, that the fact of a work of this philosophical and abstract character being written by a lady, is a circumstance which tends also to invest it with more than a common interest. The attempt itself at the production of such a work, is proof of a high degree of elevation of intellect and power of abstract thought; and if the execution of the plan be not found commensurate with its conception, the writer has herself furnished the apology. Near the close of the work, she has the following remark:—"In mankind, the particular receptacle for the light of divine truth is the understanding, ‘and that for the heat of divine love is the will; so, the male is formed to excel *his partner* in the department of the understanding, and consequent reception of divine wisdom; and the female to be distinguished by the predominance of the *love* of wisdom as existing in the male. Thus, if the writer has herein given but an obscure and very imperfect sketch of the philosophical principles, which form the basis of a glorious system of divine truth,—it is, that its heavenly image has been received in the *warmth of the heart* rather than in the light of the understanding; and that, to be fully illustrated, it must be transfused from the feminine heart into the masculine understanding, thence to be made manifest in the light of true wisdom."

In the present edition, a slight change has been made in the arrangement of the Chapters,—what were originally a " Preface" and an " Introduction" being taken into the body of the work, and headed Chapters I. and II. With these exceptions, and an occasional verbal correction, the work remains as originally published.

O. P. H.

GLASGOW, *November* 4, 1856.

CONTENTS.

MEMOIR OF MRS. PRESCOTT.

Mrs. Margaret Hiller Prescott was a daughter of Major Joseph Hiller, of Salem, Massachusetts. The family came originally from the town of Watford in Hertfordshire, England, whence an ancestor, Joseph Hiller, emigrated to America, in the year 1677, and settled at Boston. The father of the subject of this sketch removed, early in life, to Salem, where he married Margaret Cleveland. Six children were born to them, five daughters and a son : Margaret was the third child.

She was born in July, 1775, in the State of Connecticut, whither her mother had retired from the dangers of the Revolutionary War, then just commencing.

From her earliest childhood, Mrs. Prescott was remarkable for her feelings of piety and habits of devotion. She would go alone through storms to church on the Sabbath, rather than miss the services of public worship. She was equally regular and earnest in her private devotions. The following

B

passages of a communication from her youngest
sister, written in answer to a letter of inquiry, state
this fact in artless yet glowing terms, mentioning at
the same time other particulars, which set forth in
a striking manner Mrs. Prescott's early spiritual-
mindedness and moral elevation of character :

"You will remember," remarks the writer, "that
I was the youngest of the six children, and that
there were two between your mother and myself, so
that of her young life I really know nothing but
that she was ever pure-minded, warm-hearted, and
peculiarly and steadily religious,—as my mother
often expressed it, 'sanctified from her birth.' She
was a strict disciplinarian over her own heart, and
tenderly active and interested in training her little
sister Lucy [the writer] to the difficult and almost
hopeless task of self-control and self-improvement.
Her habits of private devotion, so strict and cease-
less, deeply impressed my young mind. I remember
well, that a little unfinished shapeless room, in the
attic, was taken into her possession, rubbish removed
into one corner, and in the other she had fixed a
cushioned chair covered with a blanket, and a
kneeling-stool before it. To this, in the coldest
season, she would daily resort ; and, covered with
the blanket, she would enjoy an hour of sacred
devotion, reading and prayer.

" When I was about a dozen years old, although in the same family and house, we kept up a regular correspondence, for a long period. Her letters would have made a volume :—she, scrutinizing, watching, commending or reproving my daily life, my wrong or right feeling, my victories or submission when assailed by temptation, full of earnest exhortation and tenderest love :—I, drinking in instruction, stimulated to effort, or sorrowing over the delinquencies and wanderings she so faithfully pointed out, and glowing with devout gratitude for any deserved praise. To her latest days, a peculiar tenderness for her pupil continued to glow, and was often expressed with earnest feeling."

How does this artless picture of my mother's early habits of devotion, bring to my mind what I have often myself witnessed when a child! When in health, she was the earliest riser of the family; and often, when I came down in the morning, would I find her, as I opened the parlour door, kneeling before the fire, with the large Bible on the chair in front of her. And when she saw me, she would call me to her and bid mo kneel down by her side. What mere teaching, what mere precepts, could have ever made upon my young heart such an impression, as did this example of devotion !

But I have anticipated. About the time of her

arriving at womanhood, a circumstance occurred which had the deepest influence on Mrs. Prescott's whole after-life: that circumstance was her coming to the knowledge of the Doctrines of the New Church. It happened in the following manner. Her father, Major Hiller, after serving in the War of Independence, had been appointed by President Washington to the office of Collector of customs for the port of Salem, which office he continued to hold for many years. He was a man of sterling uprightness and integrity of character, and also very religiously disposed. But, though a member of the Episcopal church, his mind had never been satisfied in regard to points of doctrine, and particularly in reference to the Doctrine of the Trinity. How there could be three Persons and one God, he could never satisfactorily discern; and he longed for light upon this point. The light was on its way for him.

One Sabbath evening, calling in, as was his wont, to visit his pastor,—the minister exclaimed, as he opened the study door, "Ha! Major Hiller, I have a treat for you here. Here is a man who pretends to give a full description of the next world, heaven and hell. Would you like to read the book?" My grandfather, surprised at the minister's exclamation, and struck with the title of the book produced, *expressed* a curiosity to read it. "O, you are quite welcome to it," said the other, " I have had enough of it." Accordingly, he took the book home, anxious to see what the writer had to say on so remarkable a subject.

The work was Swedenborg's " Treatise on Heaven and Hell." He, in company with Mrs. Hiller, who was a true partner to him, and who had suffered doubts similar to his own, immediately commenced the perusal of the volume. Before they had read it half through, they were satisfied that it contained truth and *the* truth. Major Hiller at once procured from England more of Swedenborg's works, and became an earnest receiver of the New Church Doctrines. This was, it is believed, about the year 1796 or 1797.

Some of the younger members of the family now commenced reading; and Margaret, with one of her sisters, ardently embraced the new truths. In her mind this heavenly seed found a congenial soil. Her early habits of devotion and communion with her Heavenly Father had fully prepared her spirit for the reception of the New Church Doctrine of the Lord, which, in the One Person of Jesus, brings the Divine Object of worship so near to the mind; while her long continued course of self-examination and strict self-watchfulness, and combat with her own heart, had made it easy for her to accept and take to

her bosom the pure Doctrine of Life, which inculcates
the necessity of self-combat and self-conquest, as
the great means of preparation for heaven.   Her
habitual study, too, of the Holy Scriptures, her
longing to understand their full meaning, her knowledge of their difficulties, rendered most welcome
and delightful to her that opening of the internal
sense, which is able to remove all the obscurities of
the letter, and to cause the whole Word to shine
with a heavenly light.   And finally, her habits of
pious meditation and spiritual contemplation, her
frequent lookings upward and inward towards the
heavenly world, her longings to know the nature of
that state which the Good Creator had provided for
man's eternal home,—made her eager to understand
and quick to perceive the rational beauty of those
clear and full revelations concerning the spiritual
world, which the Lord, at this His Second Coming,
has vouchsafed to mankind.   In this great treasury
of spiritual truths, a new life-study seemed opened
to her; and she hastened, with all the ardor of an
enthusiastic nature, to devote herself to the investigation.   She saw that the Lord had thrown a new
and bright light upon the path of her life, and she
went forward rejoicing in its rays; and through she
well knew that many needful crosses and trials yet
awaited her, in the process of her regeneration, yet

she felt that the Comforter had now come, which would sustain her through them all.

It was a few years after this important event in her life, that she became acquainted with Mr. S. Jackson Prescott, her future husband. He was the younger son of Dr. Oliver Prescott, an eminent physician of Groton, Massachusetts, — brother to Colonel William Prescott, the brave commander of the American troops at the battle of Bunker's Hill.* Mr. Prescott, after graduating with distinction at Harvard University, had prepared himself for the profession of the law; but being unable, through a defect in his hearing, to pursue the practice, he turned his attention to mercantile pursuits, in which he became very successful.

They were married in the year 1804, and settled in Boston. A new sphere of duties now opened upon Mrs. Prescott, all of which she sought to discharge with her accustomed diligence, conscientiousness, and reliance on Divine Providence. And, ere long, she had need of all her religious trust to sustain her under trials and adversities. The loss of a little daughter, the third child, sank deep into

---

* A biographical notice of Dr. Prescott, as also of Col. Prescott, may be seen in the *Encyclopædia Americana*. The distinguished historian, William H. Prescott, is a grandson of the latter.

her tender nature: but she now found the great consolations which the pure and clear doctrines of the New Dispensation particularly afford on occasion of bereavements such as this.　Learning from those Doctrines the great truth of the Lord's perfect goodness and Fatherly tenderness,—that the one end which He had in creation was to form a heaven of human beings, whom He might bless with eternal happiness,—and that all, without exception, who die in infancy and childhood, are received into that heaven and become angels; being enabled, too, by means of the clear and full descriptions of the spiritual state given by the New Church Doctrines, to form a distinct idea of the heavenly home to which her child had been taken, she could lift up her thoughts to that higher world, that " better land,": and behold her darling in the care of guardian angels, led by them through gardens of beauty, taught by them all heavenly truth with more than a parent's power or even than a parent's love, and preparing thus to become herself an angel, a happy dweller in the heavens.　With these thoughts, she felt a consolation come to her heart, a balm to her bosom; she felt her mind altogether lifted above the thoughts of death and the grave, to life and eternity; and, in time, she was enabled to rejoice at *having been* made the honored instrument of adding one to the heavenly host. At times, indeed, tender recollections would come over her; and, years after, she would repeat, with a mother's fond particularity, the sentences and exclamations which the little prattler had uttered in her last illness. But though with tenderness, yet it was without sadness or regret, that she recalled these circumstances. She could not wish her child back again to earth; she only was anxious so to live as to rejoin her, by and by, in the heavens.

But trials of a different kind awaited her. For many years Mr. Prescott was greatly prospered in his mercantile undertakings; and, having acquired a considerable property, was about making preparations to retire from business to his paternal estate at Groton, to spend the remainder of his days in literary leisure,—when the embargo and second war with Great Britain came on, suddenly reducing him, with hundreds of other prosperous merchants, to the verge of ruin. It required all Mrs. Prescott's fortitude and conjugal devotion, to support her husband under these severe reverses. Born and brought up in affluence, he felt the stroke, which swept his property entirely from him, as one exceedingly hard to bear. At this trying time, Mrs. Prescott's religious trust, her habit of dependence on Divine Providence, her faith in the perfect love and parental care of her Heavenly Father, which, originally strong, had been so greatly deepened by the teachings of the New Church doctrines, were called fully into operation : and they were all needed. Often has the writer heard her say, that but for the support afforded her by the New Church doctrines, in the bright and cheering views and heavenly consolations which they communicate, she should not have been able to endure the load which at this time, and indeed long after, pressed upon her. And it may be said that it was her gratitude for this support and comfort, and her ardent conviction of the blessings which a wider knowledge of those Doctrines would confer upon mankind, which induced her to undertake the composition of the little Treatise contained in the following pages. For it was in the very midst of these trials and troubles that this work was written. It was published in the year 1817. How far the writer's ardent wishes have been accomplished,—how many minds may have been led by its perusal to the rich fountains of truth, whence it had itself proceeded but as a little stream,—is known only to the Omniscient One.

No society of the New Church as yet existed in Boston, and but two in the whole country, those, namely, of Baltimore and Cincinnati. There were, however, a few receivers of the doctrines in Boston, New York, and Philadelphia, and with many of these Mrs. Prescott had acquaintance or held correspondence. She also corresponded with the Rev. John Clowes, of Manchester, England. And her intelligence and zeal in the cause were generally known and justly appreciated throughout the narrow bounds of what then constituted the visible New Church. In 1818, the "Boston Society of the New Jerusalem" was formed, consisting at first of only twelve members, of whom Mrs. Prescott was one. That Society has since grown and flourished, till it is now the largest New Church Society existing, numbering at the present time between four hundred and five hundred members.

Mrs. Prescott, through her whole life, was a great sufferer, both physically and mentally. She was subject to palpitation of the heart, which at times caused her great distress, and once or twice brought her to the verge of the grave. She endured, too,— as every true follower of the Lord must—deep internal temptation. Being of an exceedingly spiritual and interior character, her temptations were of a corresponding depth and intensity. But she well knew that they were permitted for her purification and regeneration ; and she meekly bowed her head to the stroke, striving to say ever, "Lord, not my will, but thine, be done." At length, the hour of her release came. On the 4th day of August, 1841, after a period of deep distress, both of mind and body, she passed away from earth, in the 67th year of her age. The battle of life was fought, the victory won; and we are sure that she is now inheriting the promises made to those that overcome: "To him that overcometh, will I give to eat of the tree of life which is in the midst of the paradise of God;" "He that overcometh shall inherit all things." She has entered upon those heavenly felicities which the revelations made to the New Church so clearly and charmingly describe, and which she so delighted to contemplate in prospect. She has, doubtless, long ere this, found that angelic society with which her spirit was connected even while here on earth; she has entered into full and blessed companionship with the spirits of the just made perfect, her fellow-angels; she is enjoying that blessed light and warmth that flow directly from the eternal Sun of Righteousness, the Lord himself: a glorious existence of love and bliss now spreads itself before her, and she has begun the joyous race that knows no end.

RELIGION AND PHILOSOPHY UNITED.

CHAPTER I.

INTRODUCTORY.

THERE is a mode of reasoning, which has long, we believe, been more prevalent than any other in the scientific world, which is that of proceeding from effects to causes. This mode of reasoning is, doubtless, predicated on the very natural ground, that a multiplicity of effects is always exhibited before us, the causes of which are totally unknown; this world being literally and truly, in itself, a world of effects. A consequence of this mode of reasoning has, naturally, been that of endeavouring to clear the way to causes, by striving to ascertain what they were not; thus hoping, by many negatives, to discover something positive. That this is often, to say the least, a deceptive and illusory mode of reasoning, is proved by the many false hypotheses which have been the inevitable result. It has, we presume, proceeded from a radical error into which man is naturally prone to fall, but which Revelation alone can inform him is really an error. This is nothing less

than the belief, that man possesses in himself a
life distinct from that of his Maker, when he is, in
truth, but an organ receptive of life from its only
true Source. Feeling a powerful conviction, from
the sense of his real existence, that life is his own
perfect property, he is led to think, also, that his
powers are truly his own, and thence that in himself originates thought. From this belief it is easy
for him to infer, that in himself also rests the power
of discovering the true causes of the numerous
effects displayed around him. But if man would
truly humble himself, and intellectually look up
and reflect, that as there is, as there can be, but One
Source of Life—so would he surely see, that from
that Source must issue the knowledge of all true
causes; and that they can be communicated to man
by Revelation alone, though varying, perhaps, in
kind and degree. As from one cause, however,
numerous and varied effects continually proceed,
man need not suppose, that because real causes are
to be found in God alone, that there is nothing left
for the exercise of his noble powers. Believing the
fact, and looking to the Author of his existence and
continual subsistence, for the first link in every
chain, he will find abundant and delightful exercise for those powers, in deducing various particulars from one general idea; and in tracing the cause
in the successive effects down to his own natural
perceptions of the variously beautiful objects displayed in the world and universe around him.

The assertion may, perhaps, be deemed a bold

one, that "man is but an organ receptive of life from the Lord." But let us inquire, What is life? How came it into our possession? And by what means is it preserved? And the more minute, the more thorough, the investigation of this subject, the more fully, we believe, will it appear, that it is indeed an error, to suppose that man possesses any thing of life in himself, separately from, or independently of, his Maker. The mode of reasoning, however, adopted on this occasion, must be from causes to effects, and not *vice versa;* we must, therefore, commence from some revealed truth, and be led by that truth, through its regular consequences, to the result, which observation and experience point out. By this process, perceiving the truth in its fulness and power, we shall no longer doubt the propriety of reasoning thus, or the truth of the proposition, that "man has not life independently in himself." On this all important axiom, rests, we believe, much of true wisdom. But this is only one of the many portentous truths, that are now presented to mankind; and in the following pages, it is humbly hoped that this method of tracing the finger of God through some of the numerous wonders of creation, will evince itself as a true and happy means of bringing man to a more perfect acquaintance with the Author and constant Supporter of his existence, and of educing a more clear and complete system of his own nature, powers, and duties, than has ever before been presented to his

But as we have above observed that Revelation can alone inform man of the true cause and manner of his own existence, we shall probably be expected to state wherein we find the information that "man is an organ, receptive of life from the Lord." We hesitate not to say, and humbly hope we are prepared to meet the consequences, that we find it in the "spiritual sense of the Sacred Scriptures," revealed to that faithful and meek servant of the Lord Jesus Christ, Emanuel Swedenborg, who, by a regular and powerful train of reasoning, does truly and fully prove, that "God" is indeed "with us."

Long have we desired to see these important works translated from their purely spiritual into a more natural language; and thus accommodated to the more general understanding of mankind at the present day. But to the accomplishment of this, we believe, highly useful and very beneficial work, there are opposed many very formidable obstacles.

A popular cry, almost terrific in a rational age, of "enthusiast," "visionary," everywhere precedes the volumes of Swedenborg. That he was granted supernatural information respecting a state of existence superior to the present life, is noised abroad in terms of ridicule by those, who may, perhaps, have felt little interest in an inquiry into the very important object of this information. Finding this astonishing claim really made by a philosophical author, at this enlightened period of the world, when instruction from our Heavenly Father is considered so totally unnecessary, many sincere seekers and powerful judges of truth have been deterred from farther inquiry, by the immediate and premature conclusion, that none but a deceiver or self-deceived man could think of making such a pretension. Some there are, however, who have gone a little farther. In a rational pursuit of theological truth, they have ventured to dip into these volumes as they have occasionally fallen in their way. Such persons being disgusted by an apparent crudeness in the author's communications (the necessity of which is easily explained), a singularity in the style, or a seeming obscurity in the sense, have found this disgust, aided by a previous prejudice, quite sufficient to satisfy the slight interest excited; and they, too, have thrown them aside, as nothing worth. Thus, have these treasures been buried in the earth! Respecting the author's knowledge of the spiritual world, it were well, perhaps, to remember, that there have been many periods during the course of time, when apparently "new things under the sun" were permitted to take place among men. The age of external miracles has doubtless past away; but in these works is exhibited a species of internal or spiritual miracle, absolutely new and truly astonishing. An extent of intellectual information is spread before the attentive reader, far exceeding any thing that science has heretofore presented, or the human mind was capable of conceiving without supernatural aid; the truth of which information is morally demonstrated in its wonderful display. The mind of man, generally speaking,

under the blessing of Heaven ever tending upward
in its progress, is, we conceive, making continual
advances in knowledge; and every new acquisition
adds greatly to its capability of advancing.   The
revelation, therefore, now made to man, is such as
he never could have borne at any former period; and
contains such "things" as our blessed Saviour "had
to say" to the disciples, but which they, on earth,
" could not bear."

On a deliberate, patient, and thorough examination of the communications made to the world by
Swedenborg (the writing and publishing of which
in the original Latin, wholly and fully occupied
about thirty years of the author's life), such a grand
spectacle of new, yet decidedly important principles,
is presented to the human understanding, that it
should seem they need but to be thoroughly comprehended to be cordially received, and with humble yet awful admiration.   How then, may be the
very natural query, can we account for the pheno-
menon, that even simple, unlettered minds can
enter into the depths and subtilty of those com-
mandingly grand, yet exquisitely refined principles,
while the man of extensive erudition, the elegant
classical scholar, the deep-read theologian, the acute
philosopher, and the truly rational moralist, find
themselves repulsed at the very entrance of this
Mansion of Glories?   It is at this very fountain of
reasons, and this only, that the above enigma can
find a solution; and in this system we may find a
full, a satisfactory elucidation of this, and every

other species of intellectual phenomena. It is this heaven-derived power of unfolding the heretofore inexplicable secrets of the creation; of developing the innumerable mysteries with which science at every step continually presents its votaries; of tracing the blessed connection between the glorious Creator and every possible form and degree of his works, that stamps the signature of Divinity on this precious message! It is from this glorious light, which is now permitted to beam forth from the interior of the sacred Word of God, that every real part of its literal sense is now rescued from the obscurity into which a large portion of its contents was fast falling; and that it is once again preparing to become the delight, the glory, and on earth the Heavenly Sanctuary of man.

That this is not the vision of a diseased imagination, but a substantial view of truth, time only can demonstrate. But it belongs to the cool calculator, and not to the warm philanthropist, to wait for the slow progress of time to unfold the promise of new and transcendant joys to man! The living current of Christian charity circulating in the heart, strongly impels its real possessor to impart to his fellow-creatures every good in possession, or even in anticipation. But should the attainment of a great good in prospect, depend in a considerable measure on the knowledge and efforts of the candidates for its reception, how would a belief of this condition stimulate the real believer to make known the "glad tidings of great joy," and urge on his brethren the

importance of seeking for this " pearl of great price."
That such a pearl has really been for nearly half a
century within the reach of thousands of mankind,
who have given no attention to it, it may appear,
perhaps, like presumption to assert.   But if among
those thousands, can be found even one who will
now listen to the friendly information, and apply
the test of his own observation and experience to
ascertain its truth, the writer of these pages will
esteem such an effect a full compensation for this
mental effort, and offer to the Fountain of all good
sincere gratitude for such a degree of success.

CHAPTER II.

PROPOSITION FIRST.—That all true principles, springing from one only Eternal Source, must be found to harmonize with the observation and experience of the wisest among mankind in all ages.

It is equivocally acknowledged by every rational mind, that truth can have but one eternal source; yet that source, being also infinite, must emit innumerable and ever varying, because diverging rays or principles, in which that source is traced and acknowledged through the beautiful harmony by which they coalesce with and illustrate each other; therefore, though ever varying, they are never opposing, like light and darkness, black and white. Thus truth appears to man in infinitely diversified forms, exercising his powers in the investigation of its nature and its uses. We universally find that exercise produces strength: by use, therefore, the powers of man expand and increase, and become more and more largely recipient of those Divine rays which illumine his soul.

On taking an enlarged view of the state of the human mind, at the present period of the world,

who can doubt that the aggregate portion of knowledge now enjoyed, very far surpasses that which
has ever been possessed by mankind in any former
period? Ever making new discoveries, new acqui-
sitions, the old are rarely, we believe it may be said
are never, wholly lost. Thus, though there have
been periods when the darkness of ignorance and
superstition seemed to envelope the world; yet,
these have been succeeded by others of so much
greater light and information, as to unfold the
hidden treasures of the darkest ages; and prove to
the reflecting mind, that the temporary night was
only to prepare for a more effulgent day. In this
view of the subject, then, we think it evidently
appears, that the world at large, like its inhabitants, each in particular, has its gradual progressions from infancy towards maturity; who shall
say when the latter period has arrived, and that
its motion must be retrograde?

But it may be asked, in what consist these gradual progressions of the world? We answer, in
the discovery and application of apparently new
principles, or additional rays of truth. Is it
queried, how we ascertain that these principles
have not been known and lost? We answer, that
no principles of truth can be absolutely new in themselves, being from an eternal and self-existent fountain; but that some of them may, even now, be new
to the mind of man, is, we think, morally proved,
by the order and tenacity of that mind in seizing
and retaining any degree of real knowledge; also,

in our love of diffusing or imparting our mental ~~acquisitions.~~

There are, in individuals, widely different and even opposite motives for this desire; but the result is the same, that of increasing the aggregate of human knowledge. Is it farther inquired, how we distinguish and ascertain the true from the false principles, many of which, we are informed, are abroad in the world? We answer, that true principles are fixed and substantial; the false are ever changing and illusory. The true will thus be found to coincide and harmonize with those already known and acknowledged by the observation and experience of the wisest among mankind; while the false are examined and rejected at the same

PROPOSITION SECOND.—Whenever, therefore, the ardent intellect of industrious man discovers principles apparently new, they may be fairly tried by an appeal to the enlightened understanding of his fellow-men, and will deservedly stand or fall by the decision consequent on such an appeal.

If, then, all true principles spring from one source, we have only to inquire, when new principles present themselves, whether they bear the stamp of this Almighty Hand. And to determine this important point, they must be submitted to the critical ordeal of the collected wisdom of all past ages. Mankind, then, are to sift, to analyze, and to explore such principles, to examine their inmost nature and tendency; to try them by oppo-

new combinations of thought are continually presenting new results, is also, we presume, beyond a
doubt. What, then, of the novel and wonderful
may not be offered to our consideration, it is impos-
sible to say. It is time, we may conclude, to resign
the puerile habit of circumscribing the range of
human intellect,—of limiting that, which in its
essence is illimitable, as partaking the nature of
its infinite source. Much real humility, then, and
patient investigation are necessary to the success of
every sincere inquirer after important truths. The
impatient desire to arrive at conclusions before the
premises are thoroughly examined, weighed, and '
understood, is too natural to the human mind; and
is continually preventing deductions, which might
be just, decisive, and therefore permanent. To
"learn to wait," is one of the hardest lessons given
to man; yet nothing can be done well which is
done impatiently. As the perception and acknowledgment, or the rejection or neglect of substantial
principles of truth, is a most momentous concern in
the life of man, it surely behoves him to be cau-
tiously on his guard, whenever his attention is
turned to this portentous work. That the present
is a period of this nature, is known to thousands,
in various parts of the world, who have been blessed
with the ability and inclination to examine and
thence perceive the solid foundation of those principles. But how to produce in others that mental
state of calm, candid, humble, and patient inquiry,
which is absolutely necessary, as preparatory to

such a perception, is the subject of doubt and difficulty.

That the spirit of the Supreme is the only effectual operator in this blessed work, we well know. But that the Divine blessing must descend through human, voluntary instruments, is no less certain; and that himself may be thus honoured, is the ardent though humble desire of every sincere recipient of Divine truth.

That there are apparently new and highly important principles unfolded by Emanuel Swedenborg, can be known only to those who have thoroughly explored the invaluable treasures of spiritual truth which he has presented to the world. To those, this fact is beyond all doubt. But it would be of no use to any one to believe this upon the assertion of others, as such persons would rest on human authority, which is no actual belief of the mind. This can be useful, indeed, so far as to dispose the mind to patient research; and proportionate to this, where no other impediment arises, will be the degree of success in obtaining a rational conviction of the understanding respecting those principles. To mankind at large, however, they were, by their author, conscientiously submitted. They are now passing the ordeal of human investigation. Persons of all degrees of mind, from the most simple and unlearned to the most highly cultivated and intelligent, are earnestly desired " to pause, to ponder," to sift and to weigh them; only remembering the deep solemnity of the work, and the importance of imploring for themselves the gracious aid of a spirit of candour, humility, and firm rationality in this interesting investigation. By the final decision of mankind, which must be consonant with that of the Supreme, they must necessarily stand or fall. If .they diffuse, indeed, the glorious rays of Divine truth, "the gates of hell cannot prevail against them." The mind of man will be gradually prepared to receive and reflect them, by gratitude, obedience, and joy, with all their delightful train of effects. If they are the works of darkness, they will soon be overthrown and destroyed for ever.

One object is contemplated by the writer of this little work, which, if accomplished, will serve, it is hoped, as a preparatory step to many rational minds in the investigation of these works. The system, it is well known, is professedly a religious one. Its object is to raise its votary to a high degree of excellence in religious knowledge, conduct, and worship. But religious exaltation, has ever, heretofore, been of so doubtful, and therefore dangerous a character! Its pretended foundations,—that wild superstition, which disgraces the pages of ecclesiastical history; that cruel fanaticism, which had well nigh given a death-blow to Christianity,—these, its foundations, have been so baseless, if we may be allowed the expression, and it has reared a superstructure, in the monastic life, so grotesque and useless, so gloomy and deformed, that it has left on the minds of all spectators disgust and abhorrence, or contempt. How, then, are we to

prove that we shall exhibit a more substantial or
life-breathing form of holy symmetry? How (to
change the figure) shall we prove that ours is a
"city not made with hands, whose Maker and
Builder is God?" We can do it only by showing
and explaining in what manner "God's footstool is
the earth; that His holy City, the New Jerusalem,
hath its foundations here; that the solid principles
of pure and.genuine philosophy form the eternal
basis on which it rests; and that those principles of
philosophy will be more and more confirmed and
consolidated in the mind, the more minute and closer
the investigation of every reasoning inquirer. In
order to this, then, we would once more observe,
that the object of the present undertaking is to
collect and place in a prominent point of view, the
peculiar philosophical principles which really constitute this foundation of the New Jerusalem Church;
and to show, by the blessing of God, that they are,
indeed, a full and sufficiently substantial foundation,
on which the eternal hope of man may rest.

CHAPTER III.

"Can man, by searching, find out God?"

IT has already been intimated in the introductory chapter, that right reasoning must proceed from causes to effects; that causes, existing alone in the Supreme Being, must be made known to man by revelation. It being now thus made known, that the glory which for ever emanates from and surrounds the Eternal Being, forms really and substantially a Spiritual Sun, which warms and irradiates the intellectual creation,—we find, clearly deduced from this truth, the following rational result: that the heat flowing from this Sun is in its essence divine love; and the light, divine wisdom. That from this spiritual light and heat, the natural or material sun, with its light and heat, solely derives its power and efficacy.

That all worlds, or combinations of worlds in systems, derive their existence and subsistence from one eternal and infinite source, is acknowledged by every rational mind. For, surely, if there ever existed a real atheist, he must be either wholly

destitute of understanding, or possess one so blinded
or perverted, as to be wholly useless on this subject.
That the sun of our system has, then, the same
derivation and continual support, is beyond a doubt;
but in what manner this wonderful work is accomplished, is a problem, which has ever been deemed
beyond the power of the human intellect to solve,
or the human understanding to conceive.   And if
they have gone one step farther than a mere knowledge of the sun's origin, and said, it is done by the
word of God's power, the same question "how?" re-
curs, and brings the subject to the same issue.   Has
there not been a period in the life of man (that
period when the Copernican system was first presented to the world), when it was thought a difficulty of perhaps equal magnitude to reconcile the
sun's apparent motion and real rest?   Yet it is now
as generally received and understood as any principle of common knowledge.   That the sun was created
a perfect type, an imitator, as it were, of its glorious Author, and like the hand of a dial, constantly
guided by, and pointing out His movements, is, we
humbly undertake to support, a truth which may
be proved by the philosophical principles, that are,
by Emanuel Swedenborg, first presented to the com-
prehension of man.   We say philosophical principles, because upon these premises is raised a system,
apparently new, which must necessarily stand or
fall with them.   Therefore, whether this be a true
or false philosophy, is the point to be now decided
by cool examination.

That the specific nature of heat and light, flowing
from the sun's body, and meeting our senses of feel—
ing and sight, has never been fully comprehended
by man in his fallen state, will, we trust, be unequi-
vocally acknowledged. But as there are, at present, in the human mind, many obstacles to the
reception of truth, it will not, perhaps, be so readily
granted that this natural heat and light solely
derive their nature, their specific power and efficacy, from spiritual heat and light, which are
essential love and wisdom, flowing continually from
the Supreme Being: in other words, that from the
Supreme Being constantly flows, or emanates, a
glorious sphere of light and heat, which, in their
essence, are divine love and wisdom, whence origi-
nate the power and efficacy of the light and heat
of the natural or material sun, thus created a type,
and reflecting back, by perfect correspondence, the
image of its great Original. Is not this, we would
humbly ask, a clear and satisfactory elucidation of
the important, but hitherto mysterious and lately
disputed union of spirit and matter? "God is a
Spirit," saith the Word of truth. It is the nature
of spirit, if we may so speak, to diffuse itself. This
diffusion causes a sphere of glory around the Supreme Being. The emanating sphere of this glorious spirit, then, forming and operating in and
through the material suns of the various natural
systems, produced, and constantly supports in existence, the wonderful creation: thus descending,
by degrees, from the Great First Cause, to the

lowest extreme of external nature. In this descent, we perceive that various degrees of spirit find their abode in various forms of matter.

This conception of a sphere, together with that of spiritual degrees, form two of the new and important principles, which are, in this age, first presented to the test of human wisdom. Let us hope, then, that they will be brought to an open, candid, and thorough examination; that they may be duly appreciated, and take their final station, accordingly, in the circle of knowledge.

Who will doubt, that in the natural sun, which proximately produces and supports in existence all the wonders of this our natural world, there is a godly portion of this living fire, this self-existent spirit, this divine union of wisdom and love ?* But who but will acknowledge a vastly greater degree of this same all-pervading spirit in the rational soul of man ? Herein the principle, also, of spiritual degrees, is acknowledged; and its beautiful effects can only be known by tracing the same principle "through nature up to nature's God;" which is strikingly done by His own glorious hand, in the development He has made of Himself to man, in the works of His servant, Emanuel Swedenborg. St. Paul's three heavens are there discovered to be

---

* That the writer cannot here mean, as might at first sight appear, that there is life in the natural sun itself, is plain from what is afterwards said (p. 47), that the sun is but dead matter. The meaning intended is, doubtless, that the material sun is the first effect of life from the self-existent Spirit.—EDITOR.

D

three degrees of the spirit, or emanating sphere of God, existing in various recipient forms, which, thus receiving, transmit their reflected beams of intelligence, in ardent emotions of gratitude and love. The same glorious spirit, descending in smaller degrees, forms the soul of man, and the external perfections of nature in her three kingdoms, animal, vegetable, and mineral; giving to each its peculiar degree of life, in proportion to their capacity of receiving that emanating spirit of the Great Author of all things.

There is one more important principle, which is so linked or interwoven with the two above-mentioned, that we find ourselves under the necessity of touching on that also, before we attempt to explain more fully or to illustrate either. This is the principle of correspondence, which, in its development, forms a most striking and positive moral proof, that the whole creation, as it springs from its fountain, the Deity, is a legitimate effect from its glorious cause, in contradistinction from a mere arbitrary work produced by an Almighty hand. We shall find, we humbly trust, in the explanation and illustration of these three grand principles, much substantial instruction and much deep wisdom. May we be blessed in the endeavour of developing them to the reception of the understandings, and rendering them interesting to the hearts of our attentive readers !

CHAPTER IV.

ON THE PRINCIPLE OF SPHERES, AS UNFOLDED IN THE COMMUNICATIONS OF SWEDENBORG.

SO numerous are the evils arising from a false idea predicated on a true principle, or in other words, from the misunderstanding of such a principle, that it is highly important to guard, if possible, against this prolific source of pain. It has, we believe, been an idea of many persons, probably arising from a misapprehension of the eternal unity of God, that the blessed Author of all creation is an "*universal one,*" or central fire, destitute of all form!" That this (as we esteem it) false, pernicious, and groundless idea, may not be encouraged by any thing that has here been advanced, we would add a word of explanation. To exclude the very natural thought, that because the material sun being a globular body, and, at the same time, a type of the spiritual sun, that that glorious luminary, which is asserted to be the fountain of life, is also a globular body of spiritual fire, we must endeavour to give, from the new revelation, some elucidation of this very important point. We are informed, then, that the error herein (which is surely a very natural one)

has arisen entirely from supposing the spiritual sun
to be the Supreme Being Himself, when it is, in
reality, only that emanating sphere of His divine
and essential constituents, love and wisdom; as the
material sun's light and heat are not the real body,
but only an emanation from it. Now, let any reflecting and rational man inquire of himself, if, in
the inmost thought of his soul, he can conceive of a
God without a form! Can he even try to fix his
thought on any possible thing, without its immediately presenting itself to his intellectual vision,
in a form? Can any essence exist without a form?
Does it not, then, appear almost like profanity, to
imagine the Deity in a globular or any other form
than the human? If we cannot think intently on
God without imagining him in a form,—if the human
is the most perfect form ever presented to our
imaginations, and we are continually, in the Word
of God, enjoined to "keep God always before our
eyes," how can we obey this divine injunction, but
by thinking of him as a Divine Human Being?
Can it be conceived possible, that supreme wisdom,
which embraces every variety and degree of knowledge, could exist and operate the wonderful works
of creation, without the various instrumental powers
with which man, in humble imitation of his Maker,
brings that knowledge into action or use? Can it
be possible to believe, that perfect, divine love,
which is surely a complex source of all the bene-
volent affections, can exist and diffuse itself over
creation, without form, or in any other than that of

a Divine Human form? That the common sense of man acknowledges this essential truth, and proclaims it, is, in a measure, proved by the manner of worship and address to Him, from the people of all nations and ages. Do we not universally ascribe to Him, as the Parent of creation, all the powers, both intellectual and personal, which properly belong to man? Yet knowing Him to be infinite and eternal, the "Alpha and Omega," "without beginning of days or end of years," we cannot doubt, that our derivation from Him as a parent, and our subsistence in and through Him as children, must be of a kind altogether different from our natural conceptions on these subjects. Accordingly we find, on investigation, that between spiritual and natural ideas there is this wide difference: natural conceptions are all confined within the narrow bounds of space and time, and do not rise to any thing of spirit: whereas spiritual conceptions do not admit into them any thing of time or space. We can neither measure or weigh, literally, a thought or feeling. For we can instantaneously, or in no time, extend any object of mental vision to immensity, or reduce it to extreme minuteness. Thus we must raise our ideas above nature, with its time and space, into the regions of spiritual light and life, before we can form any just conception of the "Father of our spirits," who is himself a Spirit; and to approach and resemble whom, we must worship Him in "spirit and in truth." It may here be observed, that were the Supreme Being conceived to be in any other than a human form, we should, doubtless, use the neuter and not the masculine gender in our terms of address to him. As we can form no conception, then, of a gloriously good, and greatly intelligent, Being, in any other than a human form, and as in his Holy Word it is distinctly asserted, that " God made man in his own image and likeness," it is surely reasonable, it is surely consonant with true wisdom, to imagine and believe the Supreme Being to be in a Divinely Human form. In what various and wonderful respects the divine transcends the merely natural human, is a subject too vast for our present consideration; we wish only to show, that it harmonizes with the highest wisdom of all past ages, and is, therefore, worthy to be considered as established on the firm ground of undisputed truth.

Respecting, however, the blessed sun of the spiritual world, the glorious sphere of divinely united love and wisdom, which is for ever emanating from the Deity, we would make some further observations. It is, we believe, a well known and established fact in natural philosophy, that there is constantly emitted from every created body a somewhat of itself, which finds a recipient in the atmosphere that encompasses the earth, and there produces its degree of use.

That this emission and this consequent use are drawn forth by the benign influence of the sun's light and heat, is also well known and acknowledged. In this natural fact we behold a striking, powerful, and interesting emblem or type, and, we think, a beautiful illustration of the existence and eternal operation of the spiritual sun, which, ever diffusing its glorious rays, by its vivifying influence of love and wisdom, or spiritual light and heat, gives life and activity, with the consequent power of exertion, to every created being. But as the material sun receives the very power of performing its uses in the natural world, from the glorious sun of the spiritual world, there is between the two luminaries this all-important distinction, that the spiritual sun is replete with perfect life, because God dwells in its centre; while the natural sun, having only the appearance of life, is in itself mere matter, or perfect death. In all things which are proximately brought into life, and supported in existence by the natural sun, there is only apparent life, but real death; but in all things which are created and upheld by the immediate influence of the spiritual sun, there is a principle of eternal life. The very atmosphere of the spiritual world, flowing from the fountain of life, and being consequently spiritual, is the means of supporting spiritual life in its recipients; as the atmosphere of the natural world is a means of the existence and subsistence of its natural inhabitants. In man, indeed, while existing on the natural earths, are united the opposite principles of the two suns, which are life and death, spirit and matter, soul and body. As the original constituent principles of spiritual life are love and wisdom, so the absence of these is spiritual

death.   As the pervading influence of the na
sun's light and heat extends even to the centre
various earths over which he reigns, drawing
every varied body its responsive effort towar
general good; so does the glorious sphere o
spiritual sun diffuse its benign fervors and che
light through infinitude, every where pourir
glories into the willing recipient, and excitir
or calling forth from, that recipient, a correspor
emission of its own degree of received life.   W
issues, from every intelligent being as well as
every natural body, a sphere or emanation
particular principles or degree of life, which
measure of united goodness and truth, derived
its original and glorious fountain of divine lov
wisdom, or else the same heavenly principle re
and perverted, till at length converted to
opposites.   Finding in outward nature so bea
a counterpart to this doctrine of spiritual sp
we think it not fanaticism to conclude that
founded on a truly philosophical principle.   Y
have herein given but the germ; in its fi
development and illustration it proves its ori;
the opening mind, like the sun bursting fro
horizon, and gradually reaching its glorious ze

CHAPTER V.

WE are also informed, that "there are three degrees of two kinds," viz., three degrees of love and three of wisdom, which, flowing from their Divine Author, are, if we may so speak, "distinctly one;" as the divine love and the divine wisdom, which, inconvertible into each other, and therefore eternally distinct, are yet, in their source, inseparable. That they are in a measure separated, or united in various combinations by their different recipients, will be perceived as soon as their nature is fully understood. But we must, for once, allow ourselves the gratification of using the words of our enlightened author, as none other present themselves in which we can so concentrate his highly important information. He then declares to us, that degrees are of two kinds, degrees of altitude and degrees of latitude. The knowledge of degrees is, as it were, a key to open the causes of things, and enter into them; without this knowledge scarcely any thing of cause can be known; for the objects and subjects of both worlds, without it, appear simple, as if there were nothing in them except of a nature similar to what is seen with the eye, when, nevertheless, this, respectively to the things which lie interiorly concealed, is as one to thousands, yea, to myriads. The interior things which lie hid, can by no means be discovered, unless degrees be understood; for exterior things proceed to things interior, and those to the things which are inmost, by degrees; not by continuous degrees, but by discrete degrees. The term continuous degrees is applied to denote decrements or decreasings from more crass to more subtle, or from denser to rarer; or rather to denote, as it were, the increments and increasings from more subtle to more crass, or from rarer to denser, like that of light proceeding to shade, or of heat to cold. But discrete degrees are entirely different, they are as things prior, posterior, and postreme; or as end, cause, and effect; these are called discrete degrees, because the prior is by itself, the posterior by itself, and the postreme by itself; but still, when taken together, they make one. The atmospheres from highest to lowest, or from the sun to the earth, which are ether and air, are discrete into such degrees; and there are substances, seemingly simple, the congregate of these atmospheres, and again the congregate of these congregates, which, when taken together, are called a composite. These last degrees are called discrete, because they exist distinctly, and are understood by degrees of altitude; but the former degrees are continuous, because they continuously increase, and are understood by degrees of latitude."

So luminous, to those who are acquainted with the whole of this wonderful revelation, are the discoveries made to us, by this heaven-instructed scribe, that it is hard to find in common language expressions in which to condense his astonishing communications. Yet as misapprehension, and a natural but apparently unfortunate prejudice, have heretofore closed the avenues to this exhaustless mine, some valuable specimens of its contents may excite an honest curiosity in some persons to explore these regions of ineffable wisdom; whence they cannot fail of bringing into society important additions to their intellectual wealth.

As in every thing, both in the spiritual and natural worlds, there are three degrees of both these kinds, this knowledge of degrees is, indeed, in its development, illustration, and application, a most important key to treasures, whose intrinsic value and eminent use can be known only on a thorough, patient, and candid examination. It is this examination which the writer of these pages desires to induce in the humble and pious mind; fully convinced, that the reward will more than counterbalance the labour. As there are, however, familiar to every one, many interesting and striking illustrations, which are so many proofs of the reality of this principle of degrees, it may be useful to present some of them in a point of light which will evince their derivation from it. It was intimated before,

derived one from another, in a series-like end, cause, and effect. Let us endeavour to "illustrate this by example. It is known by ocular experience, that each muscle in the human body consists of very small fibres, and that these being disposed in fascicles, constitute the larger fibres, which are called moving fibres, and that from collections of the latter exists that compound which is called a muscle. It is the same with nerves; in them, from very small fibres, are composed larger fibres, which appear as filaments, and from a collection of these is a nerve compounded. The case is the same in other compaginations, confasciations, and collections, of which the organs and viscera consist; for these are compositions from fibres and vessels variously formed by similar degrees. The case is the same, also, with all and every thing of the vegetable kingdom, and all and every thing of the mineral kingdom; in the different kinds of wood there are compaginations of filaments in a threefold order; in metals and stones there are conglobations of parts, also in a threefold order. From these considerations it appears what discrete degrees are,

tions of the thoughts and affections in the brain; with the atmospheres; with heat and light, and with love and wisdom; for the atmospheres are the receptacles of heat and light, as heat and light are receptacles of love and wisdom; of consequence, since there are degrees of atmospheres, there are also similar degrees of heat and light, and similar of love and wisdom; for the ratio (particular constitution and relation) of the latter is not different from that of the former."

The reasoning. by which our respected Author connects these degrees in external nature with their Glorious First Cause, is strikingly conclusive and beautiful; and not less so his important distinction between the two kinds of degrees; showing that much being already known in the world respecting continuous degrees, or degrees of latitude, his discoveries, or communications respecting the spiritual world, were not so much connected with or dependent on those, as on the explanation of discrete degrees or degrees of altitude, respecting which much greater ignorance prevails.

To concentrate and abridge, and yet render intelligible, the vast mass of information contained in this luminous and highly important doctrine of degrees, is a work we hardly dare attempt, yet know not how to leave unattempted. There are many deeply interesting points in theology which it embraces, illustrates, and enforces with irresistible power, to which no language but that of this Author could do justice; but which (our present

to love and wisdom, love is the end, wisdom the instrumental cause, and use is the effect; and use is the complex, continent, and basis of wisdom and love; and use is such a complex and such a continent, that the whole of love and the whole of wisdom are actually in it, it being the simultaneous existence of them. But it is well to be observed, that all the things of love and wisdom, which are homogeneous and concordant, exist in use, according to what was said and shown above."

From this doctrine it appears, then, that matter is the continent and basis of spirit. The whole system of nature, one grand effect, containing within itself its glorious cause and end. Does not this principle beautifully harmonize with that of the Spheres, a faint sketch of which is given above? Does it not unfold man to himself, and God to man? Does it not correspond with the general sentiment of the good and wise in all ages and nations, that God is in every thing?

But there is one additional and important principle, the explanation of which may throw some perhaps needed light on what is advanced above.

----

in some natural earth; and that, of course, all angels and devils were once natural beings like ourselves. This assertion opens an extensive field of argument; which is, however, but accomplishing the object of the writer. Thus, our blessed Saviour " came not to send peace but a sword on the earth."

CHAPTER VI.

ON THE PRINCIPLE OF CORRESPONDENCE, AS DEVELOPED BY THE SAME.

To explain clearly the principle of Correspondence, is not, we fear, an easy task; but that it really exists, and is a substantial and highly important principle in creation, we hope to show by illustration.

Correspondence, we may say, arises from that responsive emission of its individual degree of life, which every recipient returns to its bountiful Donor. It is that reflective power which receives and returns the image of the Great Original; which receipt and return, though ever the same in essence, are infinite in degrees and in variety, according to their infinite source, and to their recipient subjects; thus combining eternal unity with illimitable diversity. We have said above, that the heat and light flowing from the sun of heaven, the glorious sphere ever emanating from the Supreme Being, or the Divine Proceeding, called in Scripture the Holy Spirit, is, in its essence, divine love, clothed in divine wisdom, for heat is within light. This blessed Spirit, this heavenly Sun, has, in forming man, prepared two receptacles for itself, which are the will and the understanding; the will receives the spiritual heat of the divine love, the understanding the spiritual light of divine wisdom. These receptacles constitute the soul of man. When filled by the reception of the Holy Spirit, and thus rendered active, they constitute the perfect, the eternal life of man. But that they may be brought into action in this world of ultimates, something more is necessary than the mere will and understanding, for they can act only in organized forms. So far, they are only spiritual forms, and can operate only in the spiritual world or region, nor indeed even there, until they have been fixed and ultimated in external nature. They must find their correspondent receptacles in this natural world, by which they can operate here, before they have power to develop themselves in external act. In the heart and lungs of the human material body, they find this perfect correspondence. As, however, it is well known that human life has its origin in the brain, we will quote some passages from our author, illustrative of this fact in anatomy.

"That the life of man, in its principles, is in the brains, and in its principiates in the body. In its principles is in its beginnings, and in its principiates is in the parts produced and formed from its beginnings; and by life (which is the spirit of God) in its principles, is meant the will and the understanding. These two are what in the brains are in their principles, and in the body in their principiates.

That the principles or beginnings of man's life are
in the brains, is manifest,—1. From the sense itself,
in that when a man applies his mind to any thing
and thinks, he perceives that he thinks in the brain;
he draws inwardly, as it were, his eyesight, and
keeps his forehead intense, and perceives that there
is inwardly a speculation, chiefly within the forehead and somewhat above.   2. From the formation
of man in the womb, in that the brains or the head
is the first, and that this, for a long time afterwards,
is larger than the body.   3. That the head is above
and the body below; and it is according to order,
that superiors should act upon inferiors, and not
vice versa.   4. That when the brain is hurt either
in the womb, or by a wound or by disease or by
too great application, thought is debilitated and
sometimes the mind is delirious.   5. That all the
external senses of the body, which are the sight, the
hearing, the smell and taste, together with the
general sense which is the feeling, as also the
speech, are in the anterior part of the head, which
is called the face, and have immediate communication with the brain, and derive thence their sensi-
tive and active life.   6. Hence it is that the affections, which are of love, appear in a certain image
in the face, and that the thoughts, which are of
wisdom, appear in a certain light in the eyes."   It
appears, then, that the brain is the immediate receptacle of man's first principles, which are the will
and the understanding; and these the immediate
receptacles of life, which is the Spirit of God, or

love and wisdom. These first principles, the will and the understanding, are from the brain diffused through the whole body.

We will now endeavour to show, "that there is a correspondence of all things of the mind with all things of the body. This is new, because it has not heretofore been known, by reason that it was not known what spiritual is, and what is its difference from natural, and therefore it was not known what correspondence is; for there is a correspondence of spiritual things with natural things, and by it a conjunction of them. It is said, that heretofore it was not known what spiritual is, and what its correspondence is with natural, and consequently what correspondence is—but still both might have been known. Who does not know that affection and thought are spiritual, and thence that all things of affection and thought are spiritual? Who does not know that action and speech are natural, and thence that all things of action and speech are natural? Who does not know that affection and thought, which are spiritual, cause a man to act and speak? Who may not thence know what correspondence is, of things spiritual with things natural? Does not thought cause the tongue to speak; and affection together with thought cause the body to act? They are two distinct things: I can think and not speak, I can will and not act; and it is known that the body does not think and will, but that the thought falls into speech, and the will into action. Does not affection shine forth in

the face, and present therein a type of itself. This
every one knows. Is not the affection, considered
in itself spiritual, and the changes of the face, which
are also called the countenance, natural? Who
might not thence have concluded that there is a correspondence, and consequently that there is correspondence of all things of the mind with all things
of the body? And forasmuch as all things of the
mind have relation to affection and thought, or
what is the same, to the will and the understanding, and all things of the body to the heart and the
lungs, that there is a correspondence of the will
with the heart, and of the understanding with the
lungs. That such things have not been known,
although they might have been known, is by reason,
that man was become so external, that he would
acknowledge nothing but what was natural. This
was the delight of his love (or the delight of his
heart), and thence the delight of his understanding;
wherefore to elevate his thoughts above the natural
principle to any thing spiritual separate from the
natural, was unpleasant to him; therefore he could
not think otherwise from his natural love and delight, than that the spiritual principle was a purer
natural principle, and that correspondence was a
somewhat flowing in by continuity, yea, the mere
natural man cannot think any thing separate from
what is natural, this to him being nothing. A
farther reason why these things have not heretofore
been seen and known, is because all things of religion, which are called spiritual, have been removed

out of the sight of man by this dogma received in the whole Christian world, that things theological, which are spiritual, and which the councils and leaders of the church have concluded upon, are blindly to be believed, because, say they, they transcend the understanding." "The correspondence of the will and the understanding with the heart and the lungs cannot be nakedly confirmed, that is, by things rational alone, but they may by effects; the case herein is similar as with the causes of things; these, indeed, may be seen rationally, but not clearly, except by effects, for the causes are in the effects and give themselves to be seen through them; neither does the mind, before seeing effects, confirm itself concerning causes: the effects of this correspondence shall be delivered in what follows."

To accompany our Author through these various effects, by which alone his doctrine can be fully proved and enforced, would require that deep interest in the subject, which they only who know its importance could be expected to feel. But as some few striking illustrations of the operations of the principle in general may be selected, we will endeavour to perform this service. Though we have, in the above quotations, attempted to show the existence of the principle of correspondence in its particular operation between the soul and body of man; yet, as hinted previously to these quotations, its origin is in the Supreme Being, thence descending and forming the conjunctive power, through the various degrees of altitude, from the

Divine Head to the feet or extreme of creation, the natural earths, said in Scripture to be "God's footstool;" which extreme is forever protracting, that is, beings in the natural worlds are forever increasing in number, in correspondence with the eternal emanation of divine love from its glorious fountain. Our Author himself has somewhere an observation to this effect, that particulars are so numerous and so various, as sometimes to confuse the mind ; and that it is therefore occasionally better to explain a subject by universals only, leaving the particulars of those universals to some more appropriate opportunity. For it is an important truth among those unfolded by Emanuel Swedenborg, that the Divine is the same in the greatest or most comprehensive, and in the most minute particular of the creation ; and this is surely consistent with the perception of every pious and reflecting mind, which acknowledges the same blessed hand as fully in the leaf of a plant as in the starry heavens.

There can be no correspondence in the creation more deeply interesting to man, than that which subsists between the Omnipotent Creator and himself. Yet that there is such a correspondence is generally proved by the acknowledgment of the wise and good, that "in Him we live, move, and have our being;" that "from Him cometh down every good and perfect gift;" and that to Him is due from man all the gratitude, obedience, and love of loyal subjects to their true and perfect King. But, of even this very general view of the corres-

pondence of man with the Deity, little we believe
is really understood. We acknowledge, indeed, the
truth, that "in God we live, move, and have our
being;" but this acknowledgment is made not so
much because we see with the understanding that
it is so, as because we perceive that we cannot up-
hold ourselves in life or health, or without divine
aid procure for ourselves those things which are
requisite for our support. But we will endeavour
to show, by the clear light of reason, that the
thing is really as piety teaches us to believe. We
have somewhere before glanced at the primary
and important truth, that God is in form a Man.
On a clear and decided perception of this truth so
much depends, that we cannot proceed without
endeavouring to illustrate it in the language of our
excellent Author :

"Of how great importance it is to have a just
idea of God, may appear from this consideration,
that the idea of God constitutes the inmost thought
of all those who have any religion, for all things of
religion and divine worship have respect to God :
and inasmuch as God is universally and particularly
in all things of religion and worship, therefore unless it be a just idea of God, no communication can
be given with the heavens : hence it is, that in the
spiritual world every nation has its place according to its idea of God as Man for in this and in
no other is the idea of the Lord. That the state of
every man's life after death is according to the idea
of God which he has confirmed in himself, appears

manifestly from the reverse of the proposition, viz., that the negation of God constitutes hell, and in the Christian world, the negation of the Lord's Divinity." It is farther asserted and morally proved, "that to be, and to exist, in God-Man are distinctly one. Where there is an essence, there is also an existence: one is not possible without the other; for essence is by or in existence, and not without it. This the rational comprehends, when it thinks whether there can be any essence which does not exist, and whether there can be any existence but from an essence; and inasmuch as one exists with and not without the other, it follows that they are one, but distinctly one. They are distinctly one, as is the case with love and wisdom; for love is essence, and wisdom existence, inasmuch as love does not exist but in wisdom, nor wisdom but from love; wherefore when love is in wisdom, then it exists. These two are such an one, that they may be distinguished, indeed, in thought, but not in act; and inasmuch as they may be distinguished in thought but not in act, therefore it is said they are distinctly one. Essence and existence in God-Man are also distinctly one as soul and body; soul does not exist without its body, nor body without its soul. It is the divine soul of God-Man which is understood by the divine essence, and the divine body which is understood by the divine existence. That a soul can exist without a body, and exercise thought and wisdom, is an error proceeding from fallacies; for every soul of man is in a spiritual body, which fully appears after it has put off its material covering, which it carried about with it in the world.—The reason why an essence is not an essence unless it exists, is, because it is not before in a form, and that which is not in a form has not a quality, and that which has not a quality, is not any thing. That which exists from an essence makes one with the essence, by reason that it is from the essence; hence there is an uniting into one, and hence it is that one is the others mutually and reciprocally, also, that one is all in all, in the other as in itself.— Hence it may appear, that God is [necessarily in a form and consequently] a Man, and thereby He is a God existing, not existing *from* Himself, but *in* Himself. He who exists in Himself, is God, from whom all things are." The reason given, in another part of these works, why God exists in the human form, in preference to every other, is, that the human is, in truth, the most perfect of all forms, uniting in itself the highest possible perfections of all possible forms. The correspondence of man, then, with his Maker, in this most glorious of all forms, must constitute the ground of his highest excellence, the perfection of his being. Thus in God, in His form, in His spirit, we verily do "live, move, and have our being;" that "from Him cometh down every good and perfect gift," is proved in the position, "that there is one God-Man from whom all things are, and in whom infinite things are distinctly one."

of the difficulty would vanish. Were it farther understood that the word of divine truth, delivered in the heavens, must descend by degrees to the various intelligences of the celestial and spiritual regions, and thus be prepared, by correspondence, to meet its less and less perfect recipients; we should also perceive, that when it appears in ultimate, material nature, it must be so veiled and obscured by the grossness of its final vehicle, as to render its original and divine excellence almost imperceptible. We should then, too, easily comprehend why we accordingly find the external Word in this obscured and darkened state, exhibiting only here and there glimpses, as it were, of its internal effulgence. As it is believed, however, that man is formed with a capacity to rise on the scale of being in endless progression, and that his spiritual existence and subsistence is and can be alone from the source or Word of divine truth,—it may well be conceived, that that glorious Word must be formed to accompany and support him in this upward progress; that if his spiritual birth takes place, and his growth continues to such a degree, that the "sincere milk of the Word" be not sufficiently nutritious for him, in that Word shall surely be found the stronger "meat and drink indeed," which shall sustain and still continue to nourish him in that spiritual growth. We universally find, that children, in this natural world, are taught and led by appearances. They at first imagine that, like themselves, every thing has life

and feeling; and as they advance in age, these appearances, which we find variously useful in bringing forward the powers of the mind, are gradually
dissipated, and leave them in perception of the
real truth. Thus the spiritual life of man is formed
first by appearances of truth in the natural or literal
sense of the Scriptures; which, however, is broken,
desultory, and sometimes enigmatical, that this
growing mind may be excited to search deep and
more deeply.

Above, or through the merely literal sense, is
generally perceived, by the reflecting mind, a more
rational and refined meaning or train of sentiment,
from which spring the innumerable variety of doctrines, or different combinations of tenets, which
form the various sects that have filled the religious
world. This variety of construction must probably
continue, in conformity to the different views of
mankind, till the literal or external sense is universally found and believed to be only the natural
covering or body, containing a soul or spirit, according to the information of our blessed Saviour:
" Hear my words, for they are spirit and they are
life." The spiritual sense of the Scriptures, however, far from treating of the illusory and changing
scenes and objects of this momentary existence (as
the literal sense surely does), opens, unfolds, and
explains the formation, birth, and mode of existence
of the spiritual man, the true church of God;
which, together with the progress of this spiritual
man through the states of infancy and childhood to

maturity, is nothing less than the regeneration or new birth and life, which our Saviour informs us, in literal language, must take place in every individual, before he can see the kingdom of heaven. Thus this spiritual sense of the Word feeds the hungry and satisfies the thirsty soul, with the heavenly food and drink of eternal life, the knowledge and power to practise goodness in truth. Ever thus enlarging the views and exalting the mind, by instructing it in the substantial principles of spiritual wisdom, its wonders and delights have "not entered into the heart of the merely natural, man to conceive;" but with an indistinct hope of which, the truly pious mind has been and ever will be supported and upheld, through the soul-searching scenes of this probationary state. As truths are, then, we conceive, a foundation, "sure and steadfast as their source, the Rock of Ages," it cannot, we think, but be evident to every reflecting mind, that in the knowledge and use of the glorious truths and goods, thus opened and unfolded to the strengthened soul, it shall find that solid and never failing foundation for its everlasting hope and trust.

That there are contained, then, in the holy Word, degrees of divine truth, the spiritual within, and entirely distinct from, the natural, as the soul is within, and distinct from, the body of man; and within the spiritual, the still more perfect, the celestial degree, treating entirely of the descent of our Lord into ultimate nature, and His ascent thence to His original glory, corresponding with the degrees of altitude in creation: that all these things may be, is surely conceivable;—that they really are, will, we believe, be found by every one who truly seeks with a willing and teachable mind.

One thing, however, remains to be said, which we consider highly important. As in the glorious first cause there is a holy union of divine love and divine wisdom, which exist for ever distinctly one, so, in the holy Word there is a correspondent and eternal union of goodness and truth. There is also in man the correspondent and indissoluble union of male and female;—the masculine principle more especially corresponding with truth, the offspring of divine wisdom,—the feminine principle more especially corresponding with good, springing from divine love. Now, as in mankind, the particular receptacle for the light of divine truth is the understanding, and that for the heat of divine love is the will; so the male is formed to excel his partner in the department of the understanding and consequent reception of divine wisdom; and the female to be distinguished by the predominance of the love of wisdom as existing in the male. Thus, if the writer has herein given but an obscure and very imperfect sketch of the philosophical principles, which form the basis of a glorious system of divine truth,—it is, that its heavenly image has been received in the warmth of the heart rather than in the light of the understanding; and that to be fully illustrated, it must be transfused from the feminine heart into the masculine understanding, thence to be made manifest in the light of true wisdom.

It may, perhaps, be a subject of painful speculation to some pious minds, should any such think fit to peruse this little work, how and in what manner the Christian church (which is acknowledged to have been a true church of God) can be intermingled with, as it were, and form a part of the superstructure of the New Jerusalem Church. Should the author have been so happy as to have excited sufficient interest in the public mind to induce a more general inquiry after the writings in question, such a doubt would, by their perusal, be easily and immediately dissipated. But lest that should not be the happy result, it may be observed, that as every true man, every sincere lover of God and his neighbour, in heart and practice, is, in himself, an individual church, a holy temple, in which his God delighteth to dwell;—so, we cannot doubt, will every such real Christian find himself gradually prepared for a reception of the superior degrees of divine love and wisdom, now granted to man, in this new and glorious dispensation, and thus become a precious stone in the heavenly building. May many such be daily added; and find abundant reason to join the writer in ascribing glory and honour, dominion and power, unto Him who sitteth on the throne, to the Lamb for ever and ever!

THE END.